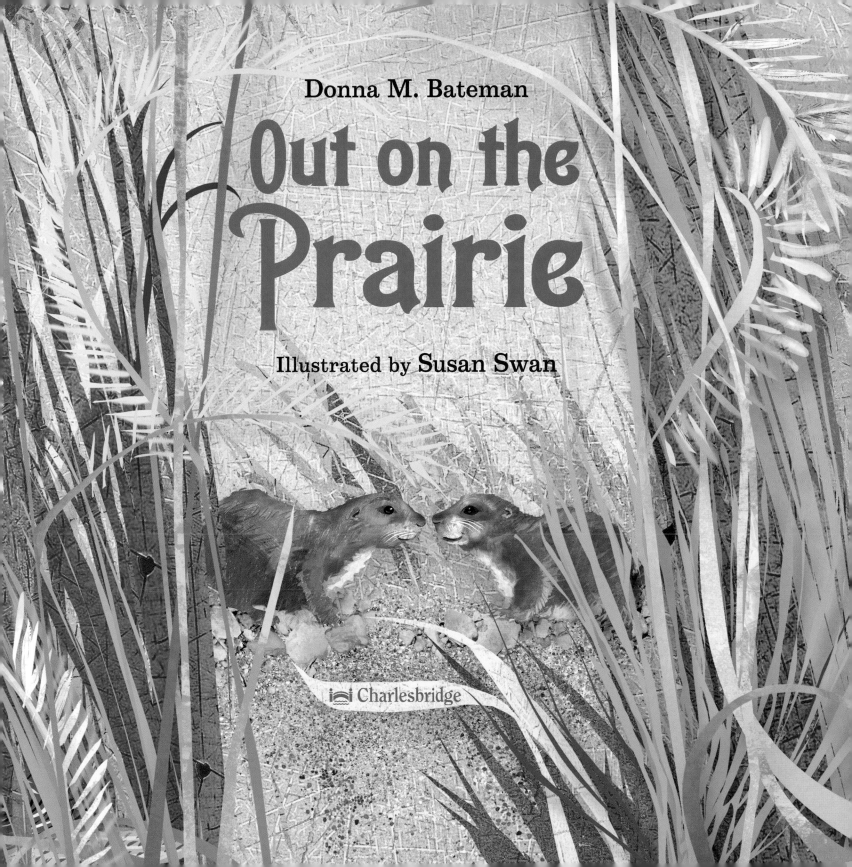

Donna M. Bateman

Out on the Prairie

Illustrated by **Susan Swan**

Charlesbridge

Out on the prairie where the snakeroot greets the sun,
Lived a shaggy mother bison and her little calf One.
"Wallow!" said the mother. "I wallow," said the One.
So they wallowed in the dust where the snakeroot greets the sun.

Out on the prairie where the sky is crystal blue,

Lived a speedy mother pronghorn and her little fawns Two.

"Run!" said the mother. "We run," said the Two.

So they ran through the wheatgrass where the sky is crystal blue.

Out on the prairie where the constant wind blows free,
Lived a mother meadowlark and her little chicks Three.
"Chupp, chupp!" called the mother. "Chupp, chupp," called the Three.
So they called all morning where the constant wind blows free.

Out on the prairie where the wispy clouds soar,

Lived a mother prairie dog and her little pups Four.

"Bark!" said the mother. "We bark," said the Four.

So they barked and they chattered where the wispy clouds soar.

Out on the prairie where the grama grasses thrive,

Lived a mother grasshopper and her little nymphs Five.

"Hop!" said the mother. "We hop," said the Five.

So they hopped helter-skelter where the grama grasses thrive.

Out on the prairie where the grass and flowers mix,
Lived a mother sharp-tailed grouse and her little chicks Six.
"Scurry!" said the mother. "We scurry," said the Six.
So they scurried after beetles where the grass and flowers mix.

Out on the prairie where the yucca grows toward heaven,
Lived a mother howdy owl and her little chicks Seven.
"Nod!" said the mother. "We nod," said the Seven.
So they nodded in the twilight where the yucca grows
toward heaven.

Out on the prairie where the primrose blooms late,
Lived a mother rattlesnake and her little snakes Eight.
"Slither!" said the mother. "We slither," said the Eight.
So they slithered, chasing lizards where the primrose blooms late.

Out on the prairie where the silver stars shine,
Lived a mother coyote and her little pups Nine.
"Howl!" said the mother. "We howl," said the Nine.
So they howled and they whined where the silver stars shine.

Out on the prairie where the moon glows once again,
Lived a mother Great Plains toad and her little toads Ten.
"Jump!" said the mother. "We jump," said the Ten.
So they jumped through the clover where the moon glows once again.

Prairie Flora and Fauna Facts

All the plants and animals in this story can be found in Badlands National Park. Many of the animals have special relationships with one or both of their parents. However, some species do not raise their young.

Badlands National Park Located in
South Dakota, Badlands National Park was named for its jagged peaks, gullies, and buttes. Its geological formations were caused by sediment deposits, as well as wind and water erosion. About half of the park, however, is carpeted with grasses and wildflowers. This grassland prairie portion of the park is the largest prairie in the United States, covering one hundred seventy thousand acres. The National Park Service works hard to protect this fragile, mixed-grass prairie ecosystem.

bison Although American bison are commonly called buffalo, the only true buffalo are the Asian water buffalo and the African Cape buffalo. The largest land animal in the Western Hemisphere, bison can grow to six feet tall at the shoulder and weigh as much as a ton. At two days old, bison calves are strong enough to travel with the herd, which consists of females and their young. Mother bison protect and nurse their calves for six or seven months. Male bison (seen here) don't help care for the young. Bison are known for wallowing, or rolling, in the dust to relieve itching caused by insects or barbed grass seeds.

clover Yellow sweet clover is common on the prairie, in small patches or blankets of yellow and green. Unlike the round flowers of common red or white clover, yellow sweet clover is a tall plant with tiny yellow flowers connected to a central stem by tiny stalks.

coyote Coyotes, also called prairie wolves, are mostly nocturnal, which means that they are active at night. They are known for their yelps, barks, and howls. Mother coyotes have litters ranging from one to nineteen pups, but six pups is the average. The pups nurse for six weeks. When the pups are three weeks old, they start eating regurgitated meat, which is provided by both parents.

grama grasses Blue grama and sideoats grama are common on the mixed-grass prairie. Both of these grasses thrive in the warm, dry summers. Grama grasses are important to the prairie ecosystem because their shallow roots hold the soil in place, keeping dirt from blowing away in the constant breezes.

grasshopper Rainbow grasshoppers are named for their bright coloring. Mother grasshoppers lay their eggs in the soil, where they remain all winter. When the eggs hatch in the spring, the nymphs dig through the soil to the surface and shed their skin. Nymphs, which look much like small adults, molt several more times to complete their metamorphosis into adults. Mother grasshoppers don't take care of their nymphs.

Great Plains toad Great Plains toads are mostly nocturnal. After spring or summer rainstorms, they mate. Mother toads then lay their eggs in shallow pools created by the rain. They lay up to twenty thousand eggs at one time, but many of the tadpoles will not live to grow into toads. Mothers do not take care of the eggs or the tadpoles that hatch from these eggs. Over a period of two months, tadpoles transform into adults.

howdy owl Burrowing owls earned the nickname "howdy owls" for the way they bob their heads. They seem to be nodding hello but are actually searching the ground for insects to eat. They are mostly crepuscular—active during twilight hours—and nocturnal. Mother owls nest in burrows abandoned by prairie dogs or other animals. The owls usually lay six or seven eggs but may lay as many as twelve. Mother owls incubate their eggs, keeping them warm with their bodies. Both parents feed the chicks. The young leave the nest at six or seven weeks old.

meadowlark Western meadowlarks are known for their calls and songs. Mother birds build domed grass nests on the ground. They lay three to seven spotted eggs, keeping them warm until they hatch. Male birds help feed the chicks and defend the nest from predators. The chicks leave the nest at eleven or twelve days old, but the parents continue to care for their young for two or more weeks.

prairie A prairie is an area of level or rolling grassland. Prairies are too dry for trees to grow, but too wet to be deserts. These semiarid lands are covered mostly with grasses and wildflowers. Prairies once covered the central third of North America.

There are three types of prairie. Tallgrass prairies are the wettest of the three and have grasses over five feet tall. They are located in the eastern section of the Great Plains, especially in the Flint Hills area of Kansas. In the western section, at the base of the Rocky Mountains, are the driest of the prairies—shortgrass prairies. Grasses here grow to two feet tall or less. Between the tall- and shortgrass prairies lie mixed-grass prairies. They are wetter than shortgrass prairies, yet drier than tallgrass prairies. Mixed-grass prairies are just that, a mixture of tall, short, and mid grasses (between two and four feet tall). Today, due to habitat disturbance, only 1 percent of native prairies exist in North America. Efforts are being made to conserve this delicate ecosystem.

prairie dog Prairie dogs are not dogs at all, but rodents. They get their name from the barking sound they make. Black-tailed prairie dogs live in burrows in social communities called prairie dog towns. Mother prairie dogs line their nest chamber with dry grass. They usually have three to five pups but may have as many as eight. They nurse and care for their pups underground until the pups are able to feed themselves. The pups emerge from the burrow when they are five or six weeks old. Although prairie dog males don't participate in caring for their pups, they do defend their family territory.

primrose Tufted evening primrose is also called gumbo lily. Its four-petaled white flowers open each evening at sunset and close again the following morning.

pronghorn Pronghorn are often called antelopes, but these North American natives are not true antelopes and instead are in a class by themselves. Pronghorn are the fastest runners in the Western Hemisphere. Pronghorn mothers usually have twin fawns. To avoid attracting predators, the fawns are hidden in high grass, far apart from each other and at a distance from their mother. For a week, mothers return to their fawns only to nurse them. At three to six weeks old, fawns join their herd with the other young and their mothers. Male pronghorns (seen here) keep to their own herds except during breeding season.

rattlesnake The prairie rattlesnake is crepuscular and nocturnal during the hot summer months. It cannot tolerate direct heat and seeks shady spots or the coolness of small animal burrows, including prairie dog burrows. Baby rattlesnakes don't hatch from eggs but are born alive. Mother rattlesnakes usually have four to twelve babies but may have as many as twenty-five. The babies are able to take care of themselves.

sharp-tailed grouse Sharp-tailed grouse scurry through the grass in search of insects, berries, and grains to eat. Mothers nest on the ground, lining their nests with grasses, leaves, and feathers. They may lay as many as seventeen eggs, but twelve is the average. After mating, the males (seen here) leave. Mother grouse keep their eggs warm until they hatch. Mothers then lead their newborn chicks to feeding grounds.

snakeroot Missouri snakeroot and Kansas snakeroot are nicknames for purple coneflowers, which plains-dwelling Native Americans used to treat snakebite. The roots of these prairie flowers were also used to treat stings, toothaches, and sicknesses such as measles, mumps, and smallpox. Today purple coneflowers, also known as echinacea, are still used in healing remedies.

wheatgrass Western wheatgrass is abundant in the mixed-grass prairie. It is the state grass of South Dakota, North Dakota, and Wyoming. Many animals eat the grass or its seeds, and grouse often nest in it.

yucca Yucca, also called soapweed, grows in dry, sandy, or rocky soil and can reach a height of six feet. Native Americans wove baskets with the leaves and used the leaf fibers for sewing. They ate the fruit and used the root juices for soap.

In memory of Maurice "Boppa" Walser—volunteer at
Wildlife Prairie State Park, Peoria, Illinois, for eighteen years
—D. M. B.

For my husband, Terry Rasberry, who introduced me to the
wildflowers and prairies of Texas
—S. S.

Published by Charlesbridge
85 Main Street
Watertown, MA 02472
(617) 926-0329
www.charlesbridge.com

Library of Congress Cataloging-in-Publication Data
Bateman, Donna M.
    Out on the prairie / Donna M. Bateman ;
illustrated by Susan Swan.
        p. cm.
    ISBN 978-1-58089-377-0 (reinforced for library use)
    ISBN 978-1-58089-378-7 (softcover)
1. Prairie ecology—South Dakota—Badlands National Park.
2. Prairie animals—South Dakota—Badlands National Park.
3. Badlands National Park (S.D.) I. Swan, Susan, 1944– II. Title.
QH105.S8B38 2012
577.44—dc23   2011025782

Printed in Singapore
(hc) 10 9 8 7 6 5 4 3 2 1
(sc) 10 9 8 7 6 5 4 3 2 1

Illustrations created by manipulating found objects,
    hand-painted papers, and scans of objects and textures
    in Adobe Photoshop to create new patterns, adding digital
    paintings, and then collaging the two together
Display type and text type set in Letterhead Fancy and Belizio
Color separations by KHL Chroma Graphics, Singapore
Printed and bound February 2012 by Imago in Singapore
Production supervision by Brian G. Walker
Designed by Diane M. Earley

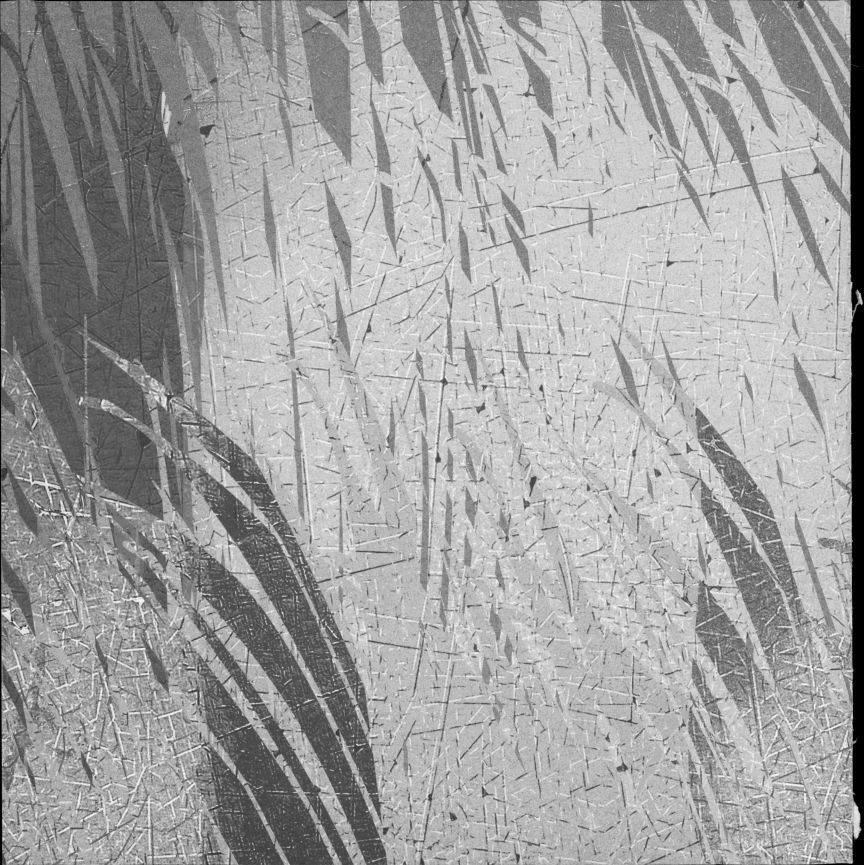